This Journey Starts With Me.

I HAVE A GROWTH MINDSET.

I AM DISCIPLINED.

I AM A PROFITABLE TRADER.

I LIVE MY DREAMS.

I ACHIEVE MY GOALS.

I see it. I believe it.

Manifest & Trade

PROOF LOG

How Do I feel?

What am I Grateful for?

What did I learn today?

What am I working towards?

What is on my wish list?

- [ ] Praticed Proper Risk Managment
- [ ] Set Stop Loss & Take Profit
- [ ] Trade Met Confirmations for Entry & Exit
- [ ] Followed Trading Plan

STARTING ACCOUNT BALANCE:

DATE & TIME:	PAIR:
LOT SIZE:	BUY/SELL & PIP GOAL:
STRATEGY:	WIN/LOSS:

DATE & TIME:	PAIR:
LOT SIZE:	BUY/SELL & PIP GOAL:
STRATEGY:	WIN/LOSS:

DATE & TIME:	PAIR:
LOT SIZE:	BUY/SELL & PIP GOAL:
STRATEGY:	WIN/LOSS:

DATE & TIME:	PAIR:
LOT SIZE:	BUY/SELL & PIP GOAL:
STRATEGY:	WIN/LOSS:

ENDING ACCOUNT BALANCE:

Manifest & Trade

PROOF LOG

How Do I feel?

What am I Grateful for?

What did I learn today?

What am I working towards?

What is on my wish list?

- [ ] Praticed Proper Risk Managment
- [ ] Set Stop Loss & Take Profit
- [ ] Trade Met Confirmations for Entry & Exit
- [ ] Followed Trading Plan

STARTING ACCOUNT BALANCE:

DATE & TIME:	PAIR:
LOT SIZE:	BUY/SELL & PIP GOAL:
STRATEGY:	WIN/LOSS:

DATE & TIME:	PAIR:
LOT SIZE:	BUY/SELL & PIP GOAL:
STRATEGY:	WIN/LOSS:

DATE & TIME:	PAIR:
LOT SIZE:	BUY/SELL & PIP GOAL:
STRATEGY:	WIN/LOSS:

DATE & TIME:	PAIR:
LOT SIZE:	BUY/SELL & PIP GOAL:
STRATEGY:	WIN/LOSS:

ENDING ACCOUNT BALANCE:

Manifest & Trade

PROOF LOG

How Do I feel?

What am I Grateful for?

What did I learn today?

What am I working towards?

What is on my wish list?

- [ ] Praticed Proper Risk Managment
- [ ] Set Stop Loss & Take Profit
- [ ] Trade Met Confirmations for Entry & Exit
- [ ] Followed Trading Plan

STARTING ACCOUNT BALANCE:

DATE & TIME:	PAIR:
LOT SIZE:	BUY/SELL & PIP GOAL:
STRATEGY:	WIN/LOSS:

DATE & TIME:	PAIR:
LOT SIZE:	BUY/SELL & PIP GOAL:
STRATEGY:	WIN/LOSS:

DATE & TIME:	PAIR:
LOT SIZE:	BUY/SELL & PIP GOAL:
STRATEGY:	WIN/LOSS:

DATE & TIME:	PAIR:
LOT SIZE:	BUY/SELL & PIP GOAL:
STRATEGY:	WIN/LOSS:

ENDING ACCOUNT BALANCE:

Manifest & Trade

PROOF LOG

How Do I feel?

What am I Grateful for?

What did I learn today?

What am I working towards?

What is on my wish list?

MINDSET
growth

- [ ] Praticed Proper Risk Managment
- [ ] Set Stop Loss & Take Profit
- [ ] Trade Met Confirmations for Entry & Exit
- [ ] Followed Trading Plan

DISCIPLINE
checklist

TRADING
log

STARTING ACCOUNT BALANCE:

DATE & TIME:	PAIR:
LOT SIZE:	BUY/SELL & PIP GOAL:
STRATEGY:	WIN/LOSS:

DATE & TIME:	PAIR:
LOT SIZE:	BUY/SELL & PIP GOAL:
STRATEGY:	WIN/LOSS:

DATE & TIME:	PAIR:
LOT SIZE:	BUY/SELL & PIP GOAL:
STRATEGY:	WIN/LOSS:

DATE & TIME:	PAIR:
LOT SIZE:	BUY/SELL & PIP GOAL:
STRATEGY:	WIN/LOSS:

ENDING ACCOUNT BALANCE:

Manifest & Trade

How Do I feel?

What am I Grateful for?

What did I learn today?

What am I working towards?

What is on my wish list?

MINDSET
growth

- [ ] Praticed Proper Risk Managment
- [ ] Set Stop Loss & Take Profit
- [ ] Trade Met Confirmations for Entry & Exit
- [ ] Followed Trading Plan

DISCIPLINE
checklist

TRADING
log

STARTING ACCOUNT BALANCE:

DATE & TIME:	PAIR:
LOT SIZE:	BUY/SELL & PIP GOAL:
STRATEGY:	WIN/LOSS:

DATE & TIME:	PAIR:
LOT SIZE:	BUY/SELL & PIP GOAL:
STRATEGY:	WIN/LOSS:

DATE & TIME:	PAIR:
LOT SIZE:	BUY/SELL & PIP GOAL:
STRATEGY:	WIN/LOSS:

DATE & TIME:	PAIR:
LOT SIZE:	BUY/SELL & PIP GOAL:
STRATEGY:	WIN/LOSS:

ENDING ACCOUNT BALANCE:

Manifest & Trade

PROOF LOG

How Do I feel?

What am I Grateful for?

What did I learn today?

What am I working towards?

What is on my wish list?

☐ Praticed Proper Risk Managment

☐ Set Stop Loss & Take Profit

☐ Trade Met Confirmations for Entry & Exit

☐ Followed Trading Plan

STARTING ACCOUNT BALANCE:

DATE & TIME:	PAIR:
LOT SIZE:	BUY/SELL & PIP GOAL:
STRATEGY:	WIN/LOSS:

DATE & TIME:	PAIR:
LOT SIZE:	BUY/SELL & PIP GOAL:
STRATEGY:	WIN/LOSS:

DATE & TIME:	PAIR:
LOT SIZE:	BUY/SELL & PIP GOAL:
STRATEGY:	WIN/LOSS:

DATE & TIME:	PAIR:
LOT SIZE:	BUY/SELL & PIP GOAL:
STRATEGY:	WIN/LOSS:

ENDING ACCOUNT BALANCE:

Manifest & Trade

PROOF LOG

How Do I feel?

What am I Grateful for?

What did I learn today?

What am I working towards?

What is on my wish list?

☐ Praticed Proper Risk Managment

☐ Set Stop Loss & Take Profit

☐ Trade Met Confirmations for Entry & Exit

☐ Followed Trading Plan

STARTING ACCOUNT BALANCE:

DATE & TIME:	PAIR:
LOT SIZE:	BUY/SELL & PIP GOAL:
STRATEGY:	WIN/LOSS:

DATE & TIME:	PAIR:
LOT SIZE:	BUY/SELL & PIP GOAL:
STRATEGY:	WIN/LOSS:

DATE & TIME:	PAIR:
LOT SIZE:	BUY/SELL & PIP GOAL:
STRATEGY:	WIN/LOSS:

DATE & TIME:	PAIR:
LOT SIZE:	BUY/SELL & PIP GOAL:
STRATEGY:	WIN/LOSS:

ENDING ACCOUNT BALANCE:

Manifest & Trade

PROOF LOG

How Do I feel?

What am I Grateful for?

What did I learn today?

What am I working towards?

What is on my wish list?

- [ ] Praticed Proper Risk Managment
- [ ] Set Stop Loss & Take Profit
- [ ] Trade Met Confirmations for Entry & Exit
- [ ] Followed Trading Plan

STARTING ACCOUNT BALANCE:

DATE & TIME:	PAIR:
LOT SIZE:	BUY/SELL & PIP GOAL:
STRATEGY:	WIN/LOSS:

DATE & TIME:	PAIR:
LOT SIZE:	BUY/SELL & PIP GOAL:
STRATEGY:	WIN/LOSS:

DATE & TIME:	PAIR:
LOT SIZE:	BUY/SELL & PIP GOAL:
STRATEGY:	WIN/LOSS:

DATE & TIME:	PAIR:
LOT SIZE:	BUY/SELL & PIP GOAL:
STRATEGY:	WIN/LOSS:

ENDING ACCOUNT BALANCE:

Manifest & Trade

PROOF LOG

How Do I feel?

What am I Grateful for?

What did I learn today?

What am I working towards?

What is on my wish list?

- [ ] Praticed Proper Risk Managment
- [ ] Set Stop Loss & Take Profit
- [ ] Trade Met Confirmations for Entry & Exit
- [ ] Followed Trading Plan

STARTING ACCOUNT BALANCE:

DATE & TIME:	PAIR:
LOT SIZE:	BUY/SELL & PIP GOAL:
STRATEGY:	WIN/LOSS:

DATE & TIME:	PAIR:
LOT SIZE:	BUY/SELL & PIP GOAL:
STRATEGY:	WIN/LOSS:

DATE & TIME:	PAIR:
LOT SIZE:	BUY/SELL & PIP GOAL:
STRATEGY:	WIN/LOSS:

DATE & TIME:	PAIR:
LOT SIZE:	BUY/SELL & PIP GOAL:
STRATEGY:	WIN/LOSS:

ENDING ACCOUNT BALANCE:

Manifest & Trade

PROOF LOG

How Do I feel?

What am I Grateful for?

What did I learn today?

What am I working towards?

What is on my wish list?

- [ ] Praticed Proper Risk Managment
- [ ] Set Stop Loss & Take Profit
- [ ] Trade Met Confirmations for Entry & Exit
- [ ] Followed Trading Plan

STARTING ACCOUNT BALANCE:

DATE & TIME:	PAIR:
LOT SIZE:	BUY/SELL & PIP GOAL:
STRATEGY:	WIN/LOSS:

DATE & TIME:	PAIR:
LOT SIZE:	BUY/SELL & PIP GOAL:
STRATEGY:	WIN/LOSS:

DATE & TIME:	PAIR:
LOT SIZE:	BUY/SELL & PIP GOAL:
STRATEGY:	WIN/LOSS:

DATE & TIME:	PAIR:
LOT SIZE:	BUY/SELL & PIP GOAL:
STRATEGY:	WIN/LOSS:

ENDING ACCOUNT BALANCE:

Manifest & Trade

PROOF LOG

How Do I feel?

What am I Grateful for?

What did I learn today?

What am I working towards?

What is on my wish list?

☐ Praticed Proper Risk Managment

☐ Set Stop Loss & Take Profit

☐ Trade Met Confirmations for Entry & Exit

☐ Followed Trading Plan

STARTING ACCOUNT BALANCE:

DATE & TIME:	PAIR:
LOT SIZE:	BUY/SELL & PIP GOAL:
STRATEGY:	WIN/LOSS:

DATE & TIME:	PAIR:
LOT SIZE:	BUY/SELL & PIP GOAL:
STRATEGY:	WIN/LOSS:

DATE & TIME:	PAIR:
LOT SIZE:	BUY/SELL & PIP GOAL:
STRATEGY:	WIN/LOSS:

DATE & TIME:	PAIR:
LOT SIZE:	BUY/SELL & PIP GOAL:
STRATEGY:	WIN/LOSS:

ENDING ACCOUNT BALANCE:

Manifest & Trade

PROOF LOG

How Do I feel?

What am I Grateful for?

What did I learn today?

What am I working towards?

What is on my wish list?

- [ ] Praticed Proper Risk Managment
- [ ] Set Stop Loss & Take Profit
- [ ] Trade Met Confirmations for Entry & Exit
- [ ] Followed Trading Plan

STARTING ACCOUNT BALANCE:

DATE & TIME:	PAIR:
LOT SIZE:	BUY/SELL & PIP GOAL:
STRATEGY:	WIN/LOSS:

DATE & TIME:	PAIR:
LOT SIZE:	BUY/SELL & PIP GOAL:
STRATEGY:	WIN/LOSS:

DATE & TIME:	PAIR:
LOT SIZE:	BUY/SELL & PIP GOAL:
STRATEGY:	WIN/LOSS:

DATE & TIME:	PAIR:
LOT SIZE:	BUY/SELL & PIP GOAL:
STRATEGY:	WIN/LOSS:

ENDING ACCOUNT BALANCE:

Manifest & Trade

PROOF LOG

How Do I feel?

What am I Grateful for?

What did I learn today?

What am I working towards?

What is on my wish list?

- [ ] Praticed Proper Risk Managment
- [ ] Set Stop Loss & Take Profit
- [ ] Trade Met Confirmations for Entry & Exit
- [ ] Followed Trading Plan

STARTING ACCOUNT BALANCE:

DATE & TIME:	PAIR:
LOT SIZE:	BUY/SELL & PIP GOAL:
STRATEGY:	WIN/LOSS:

DATE & TIME:	PAIR:
LOT SIZE:	BUY/SELL & PIP GOAL:
STRATEGY:	WIN/LOSS:

DATE & TIME:	PAIR:
LOT SIZE:	BUY/SELL & PIP GOAL:
STRATEGY:	WIN/LOSS:

DATE & TIME:	PAIR:
LOT SIZE:	BUY/SELL & PIP GOAL:
STRATEGY:	WIN/LOSS:

ENDING ACCOUNT BALANCE:

Manifest & Trade

PROOF LOG

How Do I feel?

What am I Grateful for?

What did I learn today?

What am I working towards?

What is on my wish list?

MINDSET
growth

- [ ] Praticed Proper Risk Managment
- [ ] Set Stop Loss & Take Profit
- [ ] Trade Met Confirmations for Entry & Exit
- [ ] Followed Trading Plan

DISCIPLINE
checklist

TRADING
log

STARTING ACCOUNT BALANCE:

DATE & TIME:	PAIR:
LOT SIZE:	BUY/SELL & PIP GOAL:
STRATEGY:	WIN/LOSS:

DATE & TIME:	PAIR:
LOT SIZE:	BUY/SELL & PIP GOAL:
STRATEGY:	WIN/LOSS:

DATE & TIME:	PAIR:
LOT SIZE:	BUY/SELL & PIP GOAL:
STRATEGY:	WIN/LOSS:

DATE & TIME:	PAIR:
LOT SIZE:	BUY/SELL & PIP GOAL:
STRATEGY:	WIN/LOSS:

ENDING ACCOUNT BALANCE:

Manifest & Trade
PROOF LOG

How Do I feel?

What am I Grateful for?

What did I learn today?

What am I working towards?

What is on my wish list?

- [ ] Praticed Proper Risk Managment
- [ ] Set Stop Loss & Take Profit
- [ ] Trade Met Confirmations for Entry & Exit
- [ ] Followed Trading Plan

STARTING ACCOUNT BALANCE:

DATE & TIME:	PAIR:
LOT SIZE:	BUY/SELL & PIP GOAL:
STRATEGY:	WIN/LOSS:

DATE & TIME:	PAIR:
LOT SIZE:	BUY/SELL & PIP GOAL:
STRATEGY:	WIN/LOSS:

DATE & TIME:	PAIR:
LOT SIZE:	BUY/SELL & PIP GOAL:
STRATEGY:	WIN/LOSS:

DATE & TIME:	PAIR:
LOT SIZE:	BUY/SELL & PIP GOAL:
STRATEGY:	WIN/LOSS:

ENDING ACCOUNT BALANCE:

Manifest & Trade

PROOF LOG

How Do I feel?

What am I Grateful for?

What did I learn today?

What am I working towards?

What is on my wish list?

☐ Praticed Proper Risk Managment

☐ Set Stop Loss & Take Profit

☐ Trade Met Confirmations for Entry & Exit

☐ Followed Trading Plan

STARTING ACCOUNT BALANCE:

DATE & TIME:	PAIR:
LOT SIZE:	BUY/SELL & PIP GOAL:
STRATEGY:	WIN/LOSS:

DATE & TIME:	PAIR:
LOT SIZE:	BUY/SELL & PIP GOAL:
STRATEGY:	WIN/LOSS:

DATE & TIME:	PAIR:
LOT SIZE:	BUY/SELL & PIP GOAL:
STRATEGY:	WIN/LOSS:

DATE & TIME:	PAIR:
LOT SIZE:	BUY/SELL & PIP GOAL:
STRATEGY:	WIN/LOSS:

ENDING ACCOUNT BALANCE:

Manifest & Trade

PROOF LOG

How Do I feel?

What am I Grateful for?

What did I learn today?

What am I working towards?

What is on my wish list?

- [ ] Praticed Proper Risk Managment
- [ ] Set Stop Loss & Take Profit
- [ ] Trade Met Confirmations for Entry & Exit
- [ ] Followed Trading Plan

STARTING ACCOUNT BALANCE:

DATE & TIME:	PAIR:
LOT SIZE:	BUY/SELL & PIP GOAL:
STRATEGY:	WIN/LOSS:

DATE & TIME:	PAIR:
LOT SIZE:	BUY/SELL & PIP GOAL:
STRATEGY:	WIN/LOSS:

DATE & TIME:	PAIR:
LOT SIZE:	BUY/SELL & PIP GOAL:
STRATEGY:	WIN/LOSS:

DATE & TIME:	PAIR:
LOT SIZE:	BUY/SELL & PIP GOAL:
STRATEGY:	WIN/LOSS:

ENDING ACCOUNT BALANCE:

Manifest & Trade

PROOF LOG

How Do I feel?

What am I Grateful for?

What did I learn today?

What am I working towards?

What is on my wish list?

- ☐ Praticed Proper Risk Managment
- ☐ Set Stop Loss & Take Profit
- ☐ Trade Met Confirmations for Entry & Exit
- ☐ Followed Trading Plan

STARTING ACCOUNT BALANCE:

DATE & TIME:	PAIR:
LOT SIZE:	BUY/SELL & PIP GOAL:
STRATEGY:	WIN/LOSS:

DATE & TIME:	PAIR:
LOT SIZE:	BUY/SELL & PIP GOAL:
STRATEGY:	WIN/LOSS:

DATE & TIME:	PAIR:
LOT SIZE:	BUY/SELL & PIP GOAL:
STRATEGY:	WIN/LOSS:

DATE & TIME:	PAIR:
LOT SIZE:	BUY/SELL & PIP GOAL:
STRATEGY:	WIN/LOSS:

ENDING ACCOUNT BALANCE:

Manifest & Trade

PROOF LOG

How Do I feel?

What am I Grateful for?

What did I learn today?

What am I working towards?

What is on my wish list?

- [ ] Praticed Proper Risk Managment
- [ ] Set Stop Loss & Take Profit
- [ ] Trade Met Confirmations for Entry & Exit
- [ ] Followed Trading Plan

STARTING ACCOUNT BALANCE:

DATE & TIME: | PAIR:

LOT SIZE: | BUY/SELL & PIP GOAL:

STRATEGY: | WIN/LOSS:

DATE & TIME: | PAIR:

LOT SIZE: | BUY/SELL & PIP GOAL:

STRATEGY: | WIN/LOSS:

DATE & TIME: | PAIR:

LOT SIZE: | BUY/SELL & PIP GOAL:

STRATEGY: | WIN/LOSS:

DATE & TIME: | PAIR:

LOT SIZE: | BUY/SELL & PIP GOAL:

STRATEGY: | WIN/LOSS:

ENDING ACCOUNT BALANCE:

Manifest & Trade

PROOF LOG

How Do I feel?

What am I Grateful for?

What did I learn today?

What am I working towards?

What is on my wish list?

- ☐ Praticed Proper Risk Managment
- ☐ Set Stop Loss & Take Profit
- ☐ Trade Met Confirmations for Entry & Exit
- ☐ Followed Trading Plan

STARTING ACCOUNT BALANCE:

DATE & TIME:	PAIR:
LOT SIZE:	BUY/SELL & PIP GOAL:
STRATEGY:	WIN/LOSS:

DATE & TIME:	PAIR:
LOT SIZE:	BUY/SELL & PIP GOAL:
STRATEGY:	WIN/LOSS:

DATE & TIME:	PAIR:
LOT SIZE:	BUY/SELL & PIP GOAL:
STRATEGY:	WIN/LOSS:

DATE & TIME:	PAIR:
LOT SIZE:	BUY/SELL & PIP GOAL:
STRATEGY:	WIN/LOSS:

ENDING ACCOUNT BALANCE:

Manifest & Trade

PROOF LOG

How Do I feel?

What am I Grateful for?

What did I learn today?

What am I working towards?

What is on my wish list?

MINDSET
growth

- ☐ Praticed Proper Risk Managment
- ☐ Set Stop Loss & Take Profit
- ☐ Trade Met Confirmations for Entry & Exit
- ☐ Followed Trading Plan

DISCIPLINE
checklist

TRADING
log

STARTING ACCOUNT BALANCE:

DATE & TIME:	PAIR:
LOT SIZE:	BUY/SELL & PIP GOAL:
STRATEGY:	WIN/LOSS:

DATE & TIME:	PAIR:
LOT SIZE:	BUY/SELL & PIP GOAL:
STRATEGY:	WIN/LOSS:

DATE & TIME:	PAIR:
LOT SIZE:	BUY/SELL & PIP GOAL:
STRATEGY:	WIN/LOSS:

DATE & TIME:	PAIR:
LOT SIZE:	BUY/SELL & PIP GOAL:
STRATEGY:	WIN/LOSS:

ENDING ACCOUNT BALANCE:

Manifest & Trade

PROOF LOG

How Do I feel?

What am I Grateful for?

What did I learn today?

What am I working towards?

What is on my wish list?

☐ Praticed Proper Risk Managment

☐ Set Stop Loss & Take Profit

☐ Trade Met Confirmations for Entry & Exit

☐ Followed Trading Plan

STARTING ACCOUNT BALANCE:

DATE & TIME:	PAIR:
LOT SIZE:	BUY/SELL & PIP GOAL:
STRATEGY:	WIN/LOSS:

DATE & TIME:	PAIR:
LOT SIZE:	BUY/SELL & PIP GOAL:
STRATEGY:	WIN/LOSS:

DATE & TIME:	PAIR:
LOT SIZE:	BUY/SELL & PIP GOAL:
STRATEGY:	WIN/LOSS:

DATE & TIME:	PAIR:
LOT SIZE:	BUY/SELL & PIP GOAL:
STRATEGY:	WIN/LOSS:

ENDING ACCOUNT BALANCE:

Manifest & Trade

PROOF LOG

How Do I feel?

What am I Grateful for?

What did I learn today?

What am I working towards?

What is on my wish list?

- ☐ Praticed Proper Risk Managment
- ☐ Set Stop Loss & Take Profit
- ☐ Trade Met Confirmations for Entry & Exit
- ☐ Followed Trading Plan

STARTING ACCOUNT BALANCE:

DATE & TIME:	PAIR:
LOT SIZE:	BUY/SELL & PIP GOAL:
STRATEGY:	WIN/LOSS:

DATE & TIME:	PAIR:
LOT SIZE:	BUY/SELL & PIP GOAL:
STRATEGY:	WIN/LOSS:

DATE & TIME:	PAIR:
LOT SIZE:	BUY/SELL & PIP GOAL:
STRATEGY:	WIN/LOSS:

DATE & TIME:	PAIR:
LOT SIZE:	BUY/SELL & PIP GOAL:
STRATEGY:	WIN/LOSS:

ENDING ACCOUNT BALANCE:

Manifest & Trade

PROOF LOG

How Do I feel?

What am I Grateful for?

What did I learn today?

What am I working towards?

What is on my wish list?

MINDSET *growth*

☐ Praticed Proper Risk Managment

☐ Set Stop Loss & Take Profit

☐ Trade Met Confirmations for Entry & Exit

☐ Followed Trading Plan

DISCIPLINE *checklist*

TRADING *log*

STARTING ACCOUNT BALANCE:

DATE & TIME:	PAIR:
LOT SIZE:	BUY/SELL & PIP GOAL:
STRATEGY:	WIN/LOSS:

DATE & TIME:	PAIR:
LOT SIZE:	BUY/SELL & PIP GOAL:
STRATEGY:	WIN/LOSS:

DATE & TIME:	PAIR:
LOT SIZE:	BUY/SELL & PIP GOAL:
STRATEGY:	WIN/LOSS:

DATE & TIME:	PAIR:
LOT SIZE:	BUY/SELL & PIP GOAL:
STRATEGY:	WIN/LOSS:

ENDING ACCOUNT BALANCE:

Manifest & Trade

PROOF LOG

How Do I feel?

What am I Grateful for?

What did I learn today?

What am I working towards?

What is on my wish list?

MINDSET *growth*

- [ ] Praticed Proper Risk Managment
- [ ] Set Stop Loss & Take Profit
- [ ] Trade Met Confirmations for Entry & Exit
- [ ] Followed Trading Plan

DISCIPLINE *checklist*

STARTING ACCOUNT BALANCE:

TRADING *log*

DATE & TIME:	PAIR:
LOT SIZE:	BUY/SELL & PIP GOAL:
STRATEGY:	WIN/LOSS:

DATE & TIME:	PAIR:
LOT SIZE:	BUY/SELL & PIP GOAL:
STRATEGY:	WIN/LOSS:

DATE & TIME:	PAIR:
LOT SIZE:	BUY/SELL & PIP GOAL:
STRATEGY:	WIN/LOSS:

DATE & TIME:	PAIR:
LOT SIZE:	BUY/SELL & PIP GOAL:
STRATEGY:	WIN/LOSS:

ENDING ACCOUNT BALANCE:

Manifest & Trade

PROOF LOG

How Do I feel?

What am I Grateful for?

What did I learn today?

What am I working towards?

What is on my wish list?

- [ ] Praticed Proper Risk Managment
- [ ] Set Stop Loss & Take Profit
- [ ] Trade Met Confirmations for Entry & Exit
- [ ] Followed Trading Plan

STARTING ACCOUNT BALANCE:

DATE & TIME:	PAIR:
LOT SIZE:	BUY/SELL & PIP GOAL:
STRATEGY:	WIN/LOSS:

DATE & TIME:	PAIR:
LOT SIZE:	BUY/SELL & PIP GOAL:
STRATEGY:	WIN/LOSS:

DATE & TIME:	PAIR:
LOT SIZE:	BUY/SELL & PIP GOAL:
STRATEGY:	WIN/LOSS:

DATE & TIME:	PAIR:
LOT SIZE:	BUY/SELL & PIP GOAL:
STRATEGY:	WIN/LOSS:

ENDING ACCOUNT BALANCE:

Manifest & Trade

PROOF LOG

How Do I feel?

What am I Grateful for?

What did I learn today?

What am I working towards?

What is on my wish list?

- [ ] Praticed Proper Risk Managment
- [ ] Set Stop Loss & Take Profit
- [ ] Trade Met Confirmations for Entry & Exit
- [ ] Followed Trading Plan

STARTING ACCOUNT BALANCE:

DATE & TIME:	PAIR:
LOT SIZE:	BUY/SELL & PIP GOAL:
STRATEGY:	WIN/LOSS:

DATE & TIME:	PAIR:
LOT SIZE:	BUY/SELL & PIP GOAL:
STRATEGY:	WIN/LOSS:

DATE & TIME:	PAIR:
LOT SIZE:	BUY/SELL & PIP GOAL:
STRATEGY:	WIN/LOSS:

DATE & TIME:	PAIR:
LOT SIZE:	BUY/SELL & PIP GOAL:
STRATEGY:	WIN/LOSS:

ENDING ACCOUNT BALANCE:

Manifest & Trade

PROOF LOG

How Do I feel?

What am I Grateful for?

What did I learn today?

What am I working towards?

What is on my wish list?

MINDSET
growth

☐ Praticed Proper Risk Managment

☐ Set Stop Loss & Take Profit

☐ Trade Met Confirmations for Entry & Exit

☐ Followed Trading Plan

DISCIPLINE
checklist

TRADING
log

STARTING ACCOUNT BALANCE:

DATE & TIME:	PAIR:
LOT SIZE:	BUY/SELL & PIP GOAL:
STRATEGY:	WIN/LOSS:

DATE & TIME:	PAIR:
LOT SIZE:	BUY/SELL & PIP GOAL:
STRATEGY:	WIN/LOSS:

DATE & TIME:	PAIR:
LOT SIZE:	BUY/SELL & PIP GOAL:
STRATEGY:	WIN/LOSS:

DATE & TIME:	PAIR:
LOT SIZE:	BUY/SELL & PIP GOAL:
STRATEGY:	WIN/LOSS:

ENDING ACCOUNT BALANCE:

Manifest & Trade

PROOF LOG

How Do I feel?

What am I Grateful for?

What did I learn today?

What am I working towards?

What is on my wish list?

☐   Praticed Proper Risk Managment

☐   Set Stop Loss & Take Profit

☐   Trade Met Confirmations for Entry & Exit

☐   Followed Trading Plan

STARTING ACCOUNT BALANCE:

DATE & TIME:	PAIR:
LOT SIZE:	BUY/SELL & PIP GOAL:
STRATEGY:	WIN/LOSS:

DATE & TIME:	PAIR:
LOT SIZE:	BUY/SELL & PIP GOAL:
STRATEGY:	WIN/LOSS:

DATE & TIME:	PAIR:
LOT SIZE:	BUY/SELL & PIP GOAL:
STRATEGY:	WIN/LOSS:

DATE & TIME:	PAIR:
LOT SIZE:	BUY/SELL & PIP GOAL:
STRATEGY:	WIN/LOSS:

ENDING ACCOUNT BALANCE:

Manifest & Trade

PROOF LOG

How Do I feel?

What am I Grateful for?

What did I learn today?

What am I working towards?

What is on my wish list?

- ☐ Praticed Proper Risk Managment
- ☐ Set Stop Loss & Take Profit
- ☐ Trade Met Confirmations for Entry & Exit
- ☐ Followed Trading Plan

STARTING ACCOUNT BALANCE:

DATE & TIME:	PAIR:
LOT SIZE:	BUY/SELL & PIP GOAL:
STRATEGY:	WIN/LOSS:

DATE & TIME:	PAIR:
LOT SIZE:	BUY/SELL & PIP GOAL:
STRATEGY:	WIN/LOSS:

DATE & TIME:	PAIR:
LOT SIZE:	BUY/SELL & PIP GOAL:
STRATEGY:	WIN/LOSS:

DATE & TIME:	PAIR:
LOT SIZE:	BUY/SELL & PIP GOAL:
STRATEGY:	WIN/LOSS:

ENDING ACCOUNT BALANCE:

Manifest & Trade

PROOF LOG

How Do I feel?

What am I Grateful for?

What did I learn today?

What am I working towards?

What is on my wish list?

- [ ] Praticed Proper Risk Managment
- [ ] Set Stop Loss & Take Profit
- [ ] Trade Met Confirmations for Entry & Exit
- [ ] Followed Trading Plan

STARTING ACCOUNT BALANCE:

DATE & TIME:	PAIR:
LOT SIZE:	BUY/SELL & PIP GOAL:
STRATEGY:	WIN/LOSS:

DATE & TIME:	PAIR:
LOT SIZE:	BUY/SELL & PIP GOAL:
STRATEGY:	WIN/LOSS:

DATE & TIME:	PAIR:
LOT SIZE:	BUY/SELL & PIP GOAL:
STRATEGY:	WIN/LOSS:

DATE & TIME:	PAIR:
LOT SIZE:	BUY/SELL & PIP GOAL:
STRATEGY:	WIN/LOSS:

ENDING ACCOUNT BALANCE:

Manifest & Trade

PROOF LOG

How Do I feel?

What am I Grateful for?

What did I learn today?

What am I working towards?

What is on my wish list?

MINDSET
growth

☐ Praticed Proper Risk Managment

☐ Set Stop Loss & Take Profit

☐ Trade Met Confirmations for Entry & Exit

☐ Followed Trading Plan

DISCIPLINE
checklist

TRADING
log

STARTING ACCOUNT BALANCE:

DATE & TIME:	PAIR:
LOT SIZE:	BUY/SELL & PIP GOAL:
STRATEGY:	WIN/LOSS:

DATE & TIME:	PAIR:
LOT SIZE:	BUY/SELL & PIP GOAL:
STRATEGY:	WIN/LOSS:

DATE & TIME:	PAIR:
LOT SIZE:	BUY/SELL & PIP GOAL:
STRATEGY:	WIN/LOSS:

DATE & TIME:	PAIR:
LOT SIZE:	BUY/SELL & PIP GOAL:
STRATEGY:	WIN/LOSS:

ENDING ACCOUNT BALANCE:

Manifest & Trade

PROOF LOG

How Do I feel?

What am I Grateful for?

What did I learn today?

What am I working towards?

What is on my wish list?

- [ ] Praticed Proper Risk Managment
- [ ] Set Stop Loss & Take Profit
- [ ] Trade Met Confirmations for Entry & Exit
- [ ] Followed Trading Plan

STARTING ACCOUNT BALANCE:

DATE & TIME:	PAIR:
LOT SIZE:	BUY/SELL & PIP GOAL:
STRATEGY:	WIN/LOSS:

DATE & TIME:	PAIR:
LOT SIZE:	BUY/SELL & PIP GOAL:
STRATEGY:	WIN/LOSS:

DATE & TIME:	PAIR:
LOT SIZE:	BUY/SELL & PIP GOAL:
STRATEGY:	WIN/LOSS:

DATE & TIME:	PAIR:
LOT SIZE:	BUY/SELL & PIP GOAL:
STRATEGY:	WIN/LOSS:

ENDING ACCOUNT BALANCE:

Manifest & Trade

PROOF LOG

How Do I feel?

What am I Grateful for?

What did I learn today?

What am I working towards?

What is on my wish list?

☐ Praticed Proper Risk Managment

☐ Set Stop Loss & Take Profit

☐ Trade Met Confirmations for Entry & Exit

☐ Followed Trading Plan

STARTING ACCOUNT BALANCE:

DATE & TIME:	PAIR:
LOT SIZE:	BUY/SELL & PIP GOAL:
STRATEGY:	WIN/LOSS:

DATE & TIME:	PAIR:
LOT SIZE:	BUY/SELL & PIP GOAL:
STRATEGY:	WIN/LOSS:

DATE & TIME:	PAIR:
LOT SIZE:	BUY/SELL & PIP GOAL:
STRATEGY:	WIN/LOSS:

DATE & TIME:	PAIR:
LOT SIZE:	BUY/SELL & PIP GOAL:
STRATEGY:	WIN/LOSS:

ENDING ACCOUNT BALANCE:

Manifest & Trade

PROOF LOG

How Do I feel?

What am I Grateful for?

What did I learn today?

What am I working towards?

What is on my wish list?

- [ ] Praticed Proper Risk Managment
- [ ] Set Stop Loss & Take Profit
- [ ] Trade Met Confirmations for Entry & Exit
- [ ] Followed Trading Plan

STARTING ACCOUNT BALANCE:

DATE & TIME:	PAIR:
LOT SIZE:	BUY/SELL & PIP GOAL:
STRATEGY:	WIN/LOSS:

DATE & TIME:	PAIR:
LOT SIZE:	BUY/SELL & PIP GOAL:
STRATEGY:	WIN/LOSS:

DATE & TIME:	PAIR:
LOT SIZE:	BUY/SELL & PIP GOAL:
STRATEGY:	WIN/LOSS:

DATE & TIME:	PAIR:
LOT SIZE:	BUY/SELL & PIP GOAL:
STRATEGY:	WIN/LOSS:

ENDING ACCOUNT BALANCE:

Manifest & Trade

PROOF LOG

How Do I feel?

What am I Grateful for?

What did I learn today?

What am I working towards?

What is on my wish list?

- [ ] Praticed Proper Risk Managment
- [ ] Set Stop Loss & Take Profit
- [ ] Trade Met Confirmations for Entry & Exit
- [ ] Followed Trading Plan

MINDSET *growth*

DISCIPLINE *checklist*

TRADING *log*

STARTING ACCOUNT BALANCE:

DATE & TIME:	PAIR:
LOT SIZE:	BUY/SELL & PIP GOAL:
STRATEGY:	WIN/LOSS:

DATE & TIME:	PAIR:
LOT SIZE:	BUY/SELL & PIP GOAL:
STRATEGY:	WIN/LOSS:

DATE & TIME:	PAIR:
LOT SIZE:	BUY/SELL & PIP GOAL:
STRATEGY:	WIN/LOSS:

DATE & TIME:	PAIR:
LOT SIZE:	BUY/SELL & PIP GOAL:
STRATEGY:	WIN/LOSS:

ENDING ACCOUNT BALANCE:

Manifest & Trade

PROOF LOG

How Do I feel?

What am I Grateful for?

What did I learn today?

What am I working towards?

What is on my wish list?

- [ ] Praticed Proper Risk Managment
- [ ] Set Stop Loss & Take Profit
- [ ] Trade Met Confirmations for Entry & Exit
- [ ] Followed Trading Plan

STARTING ACCOUNT BALANCE:

DATE & TIME:	PAIR:
LOT SIZE:	BUY/SELL & PIP GOAL:
STRATEGY:	WIN/LOSS:

DATE & TIME:	PAIR:
LOT SIZE:	BUY/SELL & PIP GOAL:
STRATEGY:	WIN/LOSS:

DATE & TIME:	PAIR:
LOT SIZE:	BUY/SELL & PIP GOAL:
STRATEGY:	WIN/LOSS:

DATE & TIME:	PAIR:
LOT SIZE:	BUY/SELL & PIP GOAL:
STRATEGY:	WIN/LOSS:

ENDING ACCOUNT BALANCE:

Manifest & Trade

PROOF LOG

How Do I feel?

What am I Grateful for?

What did I learn today?

What am I working towards?

What is on my wish list?

- [ ] Praticed Proper Risk Managment
- [ ] Set Stop Loss & Take Profit
- [ ] Trade Met Confirmations for Entry & Exit
- [ ] Followed Trading Plan

STARTING ACCOUNT BALANCE:

DATE & TIME:	PAIR:
LOT SIZE:	BUY/SELL & PIP GOAL:
STRATEGY:	WIN/LOSS:

DATE & TIME:	PAIR:
LOT SIZE:	BUY/SELL & PIP GOAL:
STRATEGY:	WIN/LOSS:

DATE & TIME:	PAIR:
LOT SIZE:	BUY/SELL & PIP GOAL:
STRATEGY:	WIN/LOSS:

DATE & TIME:	PAIR:
LOT SIZE:	BUY/SELL & PIP GOAL:
STRATEGY:	WIN/LOSS:

ENDING ACCOUNT BALANCE:

Manifest & Trade
PROOF LOG

How Do I feel?

What am I Grateful for?

What did I learn today?

What am I working towards?

What is on my wish list?

☐ Praticed Proper Risk Managment

☐ Set Stop Loss & Take Profit

☐ Trade Met Confirmations for Entry & Exit

☐ Followed Trading Plan

STARTING ACCOUNT BALANCE:

DATE & TIME:	PAIR:
LOT SIZE:	BUY/SELL & PIP GOAL:
STRATEGY:	WIN/LOSS:

DATE & TIME:	PAIR:
LOT SIZE:	BUY/SELL & PIP GOAL:
STRATEGY:	WIN/LOSS:

DATE & TIME:	PAIR:
LOT SIZE:	BUY/SELL & PIP GOAL:
STRATEGY:	WIN/LOSS:

DATE & TIME:	PAIR:
LOT SIZE:	BUY/SELL & PIP GOAL:
STRATEGY:	WIN/LOSS:

ENDING ACCOUNT BALANCE:

Manifest & Trade

PROOF LOG

How Do I feel?

What am I Grateful for?

What did I learn today?

What am I working towards?

What is on my wish list?

☐ Praticed Proper Risk Managment

☐ Set Stop Loss & Take Profit

☐ Trade Met Confirmations for Entry & Exit

☐ Followed Trading Plan

STARTING ACCOUNT BALANCE:

DATE & TIME:	PAIR:
LOT SIZE:	BUY/SELL & PIP GOAL:
STRATEGY:	WIN/LOSS:

DATE & TIME:	PAIR:
LOT SIZE:	BUY/SELL & PIP GOAL:
STRATEGY:	WIN/LOSS:

DATE & TIME:	PAIR:
LOT SIZE:	BUY/SELL & PIP GOAL:
STRATEGY:	WIN/LOSS:

DATE & TIME:	PAIR:
LOT SIZE:	BUY/SELL & PIP GOAL:
STRATEGY:	WIN/LOSS:

ENDING ACCOUNT BALANCE:

Manifest & Trade

PROOF LOG

How Do I feel?

What am I Grateful for?

What did I learn today?

What am I working towards?

What is on my wish list?

MINDSET
growth

- [ ] Praticed Proper Risk Managment
- [ ] Set Stop Loss & Take Profit
- [ ] Trade Met Confirmations for Entry & Exit
- [ ] Followed Trading Plan

DISCIPLINE
checklist

TRADING
log

STARTING ACCOUNT BALANCE:

DATE & TIME:	PAIR:
LOT SIZE:	BUY/SELL & PIP GOAL:
STRATEGY:	WIN/LOSS:

DATE & TIME:	PAIR:
LOT SIZE:	BUY/SELL & PIP GOAL:
STRATEGY:	WIN/LOSS:

DATE & TIME:	PAIR:
LOT SIZE:	BUY/SELL & PIP GOAL:
STRATEGY:	WIN/LOSS:

DATE & TIME:	PAIR:
LOT SIZE:	BUY/SELL & PIP GOAL:
STRATEGY:	WIN/LOSS:

ENDING ACCOUNT BALANCE:

Manifest & Trade

PROOF LOG

How Do I feel?

What am I Grateful for?

What did I learn today?

What am I working towards?

What is on my wish list?

- ☐ Praticed Proper Risk Managment
- ☐ Set Stop Loss & Take Profit
- ☐ Trade Met Confirmations for Entry & Exit
- ☐ Followed Trading Plan

STARTING ACCOUNT BALANCE:

DATE & TIME:	PAIR:
LOT SIZE:	BUY/SELL & PIP GOAL:
STRATEGY:	WIN/LOSS:

DATE & TIME:	PAIR:
LOT SIZE:	BUY/SELL & PIP GOAL:
STRATEGY:	WIN/LOSS:

DATE & TIME:	PAIR:
LOT SIZE:	BUY/SELL & PIP GOAL:
STRATEGY:	WIN/LOSS:

DATE & TIME:	PAIR:
LOT SIZE:	BUY/SELL & PIP GOAL:
STRATEGY:	WIN/LOSS:

ENDING ACCOUNT BALANCE:

Manifest & Trade

How Do I feel?

What am I Grateful for?

What did I learn today?

What am I working towards?

What is on my wish list?

MINDSET
growth

- [ ] Praticed Proper Risk Managment
- [ ] Set Stop Loss & Take Profit
- [ ] Trade Met Confirmations for Entry & Exit
- [ ] Followed Trading Plan

DISCIPLINE
checklist

TRADING
log

STARTING ACCOUNT BALANCE:

DATE & TIME:	PAIR:
LOT SIZE:	BUY/SELL & PIP GOAL:
STRATEGY:	WIN/LOSS:

DATE & TIME:	PAIR:
LOT SIZE:	BUY/SELL & PIP GOAL:
STRATEGY:	WIN/LOSS:

DATE & TIME:	PAIR:
LOT SIZE:	BUY/SELL & PIP GOAL:
STRATEGY:	WIN/LOSS:

DATE & TIME:	PAIR:
LOT SIZE:	BUY/SELL & PIP GOAL:
STRATEGY:	WIN/LOSS:

ENDING ACCOUNT BALANCE:

Manifest & Trade

PROOF LOG

How Do I feel?

What am I Grateful for?

What did I learn today?

What am I working towards?

What is on my wish list?

- [ ] Praticed Proper Risk Managment
- [ ] Set Stop Loss & Take Profit
- [ ] Trade Met Confirmations for Entry & Exit
- [ ] Followed Trading Plan

STARTING ACCOUNT BALANCE:

DATE & TIME:	PAIR:
LOT SIZE:	BUY/SELL & PIP GOAL:
STRATEGY:	WIN/LOSS:

DATE & TIME:	PAIR:
LOT SIZE:	BUY/SELL & PIP GOAL:
STRATEGY:	WIN/LOSS:

DATE & TIME:	PAIR:
LOT SIZE:	BUY/SELL & PIP GOAL:
STRATEGY:	WIN/LOSS:

DATE & TIME:	PAIR:
LOT SIZE:	BUY/SELL & PIP GOAL:
STRATEGY:	WIN/LOSS:

ENDING ACCOUNT BALANCE:

Manifest & Trade

PROOF LOG

How Do I feel?

What am I Grateful for?

What did I learn today?

What am I working towards?

What is on my wish list?

MINDSET
growth

☐ Praticed Proper Risk Managment

☐ Set Stop Loss & Take Profit

☐ Trade Met Confirmations for Entry & Exit

☐ Followed Trading Plan

DISCIPLINE
checklist

TRADING
log

STARTING ACCOUNT BALANCE:

DATE & TIME:	PAIR:
LOT SIZE:	BUY/SELL & PIP GOAL:
STRATEGY:	WIN/LOSS:

DATE & TIME:	PAIR:
LOT SIZE:	BUY/SELL & PIP GOAL:
STRATEGY:	WIN/LOSS:

DATE & TIME:	PAIR:
LOT SIZE:	BUY/SELL & PIP GOAL:
STRATEGY:	WIN/LOSS:

DATE & TIME:	PAIR:
LOT SIZE:	BUY/SELL & PIP GOAL:
STRATEGY:	WIN/LOSS:

ENDING ACCOUNT BALANCE:

Manifest & Trade

PROOF LOG

How Do I feel?

What am I Grateful for?

What did I learn today?

What am I working towards?

What is on my wish list?

☐   Praticed Proper Risk Managment

☐   Set Stop Loss & Take Profit

☐   Trade Met Confirmations for Entry & Exit

☐   Followed Trading Plan

STARTING ACCOUNT BALANCE:

DATE & TIME:	PAIR:
LOT SIZE:	BUY/SELL & PIP GOAL:
STRATEGY:	WIN/LOSS:

DATE & TIME:	PAIR:
LOT SIZE:	BUY/SELL & PIP GOAL:
STRATEGY:	WIN/LOSS:

DATE & TIME:	PAIR:
LOT SIZE:	BUY/SELL & PIP GOAL:
STRATEGY:	WIN/LOSS:

DATE & TIME:	PAIR:
LOT SIZE:	BUY/SELL & PIP GOAL:
STRATEGY:	WIN/LOSS:

ENDING ACCOUNT BALANCE:

Manifest & Trade

PROOF LOG

How Do I feel?

What am I Grateful for?

What did I learn today?

What am I working towards?

What is on my wish list?

- [ ] Praticed Proper Risk Managment
- [ ] Set Stop Loss & Take Profit
- [ ] Trade Met Confirmations for Entry & Exit
- [ ] Followed Trading Plan

STARTING ACCOUNT BALANCE:

DATE & TIME:	PAIR:
LOT SIZE:	BUY/SELL & PIP GOAL:
STRATEGY:	WIN/LOSS:

DATE & TIME:	PAIR:
LOT SIZE:	BUY/SELL & PIP GOAL:
STRATEGY:	WIN/LOSS:

DATE & TIME:	PAIR:
LOT SIZE:	BUY/SELL & PIP GOAL:
STRATEGY:	WIN/LOSS:

DATE & TIME:	PAIR:
LOT SIZE:	BUY/SELL & PIP GOAL:
STRATEGY:	WIN/LOSS:

ENDING ACCOUNT BALANCE:

Manifest & Trade

PROOF LOG

How Do I feel?

What am I Grateful for?

What did I learn today?

What am I working towards?

What is on my wish list?

- [ ] Praticed Proper Risk Managment
- [ ] Set Stop Loss & Take Profit
- [ ] Trade Met Confirmations for Entry & Exit
- [ ] Followed Trading Plan

STARTING ACCOUNT BALANCE:

DATE & TIME:	PAIR:
LOT SIZE:	BUY/SELL & PIP GOAL:
STRATEGY:	WIN/LOSS:

DATE & TIME:	PAIR:
LOT SIZE:	BUY/SELL & PIP GOAL:
STRATEGY:	WIN/LOSS:

DATE & TIME:	PAIR:
LOT SIZE:	BUY/SELL & PIP GOAL:
STRATEGY:	WIN/LOSS:

DATE & TIME:	PAIR:
LOT SIZE:	BUY/SELL & PIP GOAL:
STRATEGY:	WIN/LOSS:

ENDING ACCOUNT BALANCE:

Manifest & Trade

PROOF LOG

How Do I feel?

What am I Grateful for?

What did I learn today?

What am I working towards?

What is on my wish list?

- [ ] Praticed Proper Risk Managment
- [ ] Set Stop Loss & Take Profit
- [ ] Trade Met Confirmations for Entry & Exit
- [ ] Followed Trading Plan

STARTING ACCOUNT BALANCE:

DATE & TIME: _____ | PAIR: _____

LOT SIZE: _____ | BUY/SELL & PIP GOAL: _____

STRATEGY: _____ | WIN/LOSS: _____

DATE & TIME: _____ | PAIR: _____

LOT SIZE: _____ | BUY/SELL & PIP GOAL: _____

STRATEGY: _____ | WIN/LOSS: _____

DATE & TIME: _____ | PAIR: _____

LOT SIZE: _____ | BUY/SELL & PIP GOAL: _____

STRATEGY: _____ | WIN/LOSS: _____

DATE & TIME: _____ | PAIR: _____

LOT SIZE: _____ | BUY/SELL & PIP GOAL: _____

STRATEGY: _____ | WIN/LOSS: _____

ENDING ACCOUNT BALANCE:

Manifest & Trade

PROOF LOG

How Do I feel?

What am I Grateful for?

What did I learn today?

What am I working towards?

What is on my wish list?

- [ ] Praticed Proper Risk Managment
- [ ] Set Stop Loss & Take Profit
- [ ] Trade Met Confirmations for Entry & Exit
- [ ] Followed Trading Plan

STARTING ACCOUNT BALANCE:

DATE & TIME:	PAIR:
LOT SIZE:	BUY/SELL & PIP GOAL:
STRATEGY:	WIN/LOSS:

DATE & TIME:	PAIR:
LOT SIZE:	BUY/SELL & PIP GOAL:
STRATEGY:	WIN/LOSS:

DATE & TIME:	PAIR:
LOT SIZE:	BUY/SELL & PIP GOAL:
STRATEGY:	WIN/LOSS:

DATE & TIME:	PAIR:
LOT SIZE:	BUY/SELL & PIP GOAL:
STRATEGY:	WIN/LOSS:

ENDING ACCOUNT BALANCE:

Manifest & Trade

PROOF LOG

How Do I feel?

What am I Grateful for?

What did I learn today?

What am I working towards?

What is on my wish list?

- [ ] Praticed Proper Risk Managment
- [ ] Set Stop Loss & Take Profit
- [ ] Trade Met Confirmations for Entry & Exit
- [ ] Followed Trading Plan

STARTING ACCOUNT BALANCE:

DATE & TIME:	PAIR:
LOT SIZE:	BUY/SELL & PIP GOAL:
STRATEGY:	WIN/LOSS:

DATE & TIME:	PAIR:
LOT SIZE:	BUY/SELL & PIP GOAL:
STRATEGY:	WIN/LOSS:

DATE & TIME:	PAIR:
LOT SIZE:	BUY/SELL & PIP GOAL:
STRATEGY:	WIN/LOSS:

DATE & TIME:	PAIR:
LOT SIZE:	BUY/SELL & PIP GOAL:
STRATEGY:	WIN/LOSS:

ENDING ACCOUNT BALANCE:

Manifest & Trade

PROOF LOG

How Do I feel?

What am I Grateful for?

What did I learn today?

What am I working towards?

What is on my wish list?

MINDSET
growth

- [ ] Praticed Proper Risk Managment
- [ ] Set Stop Loss & Take Profit
- [ ] Trade Met Confirmations for Entry & Exit
- [ ] Followed Trading Plan

DISCIPLINE
checklist

TRADING
log

STARTING ACCOUNT BALANCE:

DATE & TIME:	PAIR:
LOT SIZE:	BUY/SELL & PIP GOAL:
STRATEGY:	WIN/LOSS:

DATE & TIME:	PAIR:
LOT SIZE:	BUY/SELL & PIP GOAL:
STRATEGY:	WIN/LOSS:

DATE & TIME:	PAIR:
LOT SIZE:	BUY/SELL & PIP GOAL:
STRATEGY:	WIN/LOSS:

DATE & TIME:	PAIR:
LOT SIZE:	BUY/SELL & PIP GOAL:
STRATEGY:	WIN/LOSS:

ENDING ACCOUNT BALANCE:

Manifest & Trade

PROOF LOG

How Do I feel?

What am I Grateful for?

What did I learn today?

What am I working towards?

What is on my wish list?

- [ ] Praticed Proper Risk Managment
- [ ] Set Stop Loss & Take Profit
- [ ] Trade Met Confirmations for Entry & Exit
- [ ] Followed Trading Plan

STARTING ACCOUNT BALANCE:

DATE & TIME:	PAIR:
LOT SIZE:	BUY/SELL & PIP GOAL:
STRATEGY:	WIN/LOSS:

DATE & TIME:	PAIR:
LOT SIZE:	BUY/SELL & PIP GOAL:
STRATEGY:	WIN/LOSS:

DATE & TIME:	PAIR:
LOT SIZE:	BUY/SELL & PIP GOAL:
STRATEGY:	WIN/LOSS:

DATE & TIME:	PAIR:
LOT SIZE:	BUY/SELL & PIP GOAL:
STRATEGY:	WIN/LOSS:

ENDING ACCOUNT BALANCE:

Manifest & Trade

PROOF LOG

How Do I feel?

What am I Grateful for?

What did I learn today?

What am I working towards?

What is on my wish list?

- [ ] Praticed Proper Risk Managment
- [ ] Set Stop Loss & Take Profit
- [ ] Trade Met Confirmations for Entry & Exit
- [ ] Followed Trading Plan

STARTING ACCOUNT BALANCE:

DATE & TIME:	PAIR:
LOT SIZE:	BUY/SELL & PIP GOAL:
STRATEGY:	WIN/LOSS:

DATE & TIME:	PAIR:
LOT SIZE:	BUY/SELL & PIP GOAL:
STRATEGY:	WIN/LOSS:

DATE & TIME:	PAIR:
LOT SIZE:	BUY/SELL & PIP GOAL:
STRATEGY:	WIN/LOSS:

DATE & TIME:	PAIR:
LOT SIZE:	BUY/SELL & PIP GOAL:
STRATEGY:	WIN/LOSS:

ENDING ACCOUNT BALANCE:

Manifest & Trade

PROOF LOG

How Do I feel?

What am I Grateful for?

What did I learn today?

What am I working towards?

What is on my wish list?

☐ Praticed Proper Risk Managment

☐ Set Stop Loss & Take Profit

☐ Trade Met Confirmations for Entry & Exit

☐ Followed Trading Plan

MINDSET *growth*

DISCIPLINE *checklist*

TRADING *log*

STARTING ACCOUNT BALANCE:

DATE & TIME:	PAIR:
LOT SIZE:	BUY/SELL & PIP GOAL:
STRATEGY:	WIN/LOSS:

DATE & TIME:	PAIR:
LOT SIZE:	BUY/SELL & PIP GOAL:
STRATEGY:	WIN/LOSS:

DATE & TIME:	PAIR:
LOT SIZE:	BUY/SELL & PIP GOAL:
STRATEGY:	WIN/LOSS:

DATE & TIME:	PAIR:
LOT SIZE:	BUY/SELL & PIP GOAL:
STRATEGY:	WIN/LOSS:

ENDING ACCOUNT BALANCE:

Manifest & Trade

PROOF LOG

How Do I feel?

What am I Grateful for?

What did I learn today?

What am I working towards?

What is on my wish list?

☐   Praticed Proper Risk Managment

☐   Set Stop Loss & Take Profit

☐   Trade Met Confirmations for Entry & Exit

☐   Followed Trading Plan

STARTING ACCOUNT BALANCE:

DATE & TIME:	PAIR:
LOT SIZE:	BUY/SELL & PIP GOAL:
STRATEGY:	WIN/LOSS:

DATE & TIME:	PAIR:
LOT SIZE:	BUY/SELL & PIP GOAL:
STRATEGY:	WIN/LOSS:

DATE & TIME:	PAIR:
LOT SIZE:	BUY/SELL & PIP GOAL:
STRATEGY:	WIN/LOSS:

DATE & TIME:	PAIR:
LOT SIZE:	BUY/SELL & PIP GOAL:
STRATEGY:	WIN/LOSS:

ENDING ACCOUNT BALANCE:

Manifest & Trade

PROOF LOG

How Do I feel?

What am I Grateful for?

What did I learn today?

What am I working towards?

What is on my wish list?

- [ ] Praticed Proper Risk Managment
- [ ] Set Stop Loss & Take Profit
- [ ] Trade Met Confirmations for Entry & Exit
- [ ] Followed Trading Plan

STARTING ACCOUNT BALANCE:

DATE & TIME:	PAIR:
LOT SIZE:	BUY/SELL & PIP GOAL:
STRATEGY:	WIN/LOSS:

DATE & TIME:	PAIR:
LOT SIZE:	BUY/SELL & PIP GOAL:
STRATEGY:	WIN/LOSS:

DATE & TIME:	PAIR:
LOT SIZE:	BUY/SELL & PIP GOAL:
STRATEGY:	WIN/LOSS:

DATE & TIME:	PAIR:
LOT SIZE:	BUY/SELL & PIP GOAL:
STRATEGY:	WIN/LOSS:

ENDING ACCOUNT BALANCE:

Manifest & Trade

PROOF LOG

How Do I feel?

What am I Grateful for?

What did I learn today?

What am I working towards?

What is on my wish list?

☐ Praticed Proper Risk Managment

☐ Set Stop Loss & Take Profit

☐ Trade Met Confirmations for Entry & Exit

☐ Followed Trading Plan

MINDSET *growth*

DISCIPLINE *checklist*

TRADING *log*

STARTING ACCOUNT BALANCE:

DATE & TIME:	PAIR:
LOT SIZE:	BUY/SELL & PIP GOAL:
STRATEGY:	WIN/LOSS:

DATE & TIME:	PAIR:
LOT SIZE:	BUY/SELL & PIP GOAL:
STRATEGY:	WIN/LOSS:

DATE & TIME:	PAIR:
LOT SIZE:	BUY/SELL & PIP GOAL:
STRATEGY:	WIN/LOSS:

DATE & TIME:	PAIR:
LOT SIZE:	BUY/SELL & PIP GOAL:
STRATEGY:	WIN/LOSS:

ENDING ACCOUNT BALANCE:

Manifest & Trade

PROOF LOG

How Do I feel?

What am I Grateful for?

What did I learn today?

What am I working towards?

What is on my wish list?

- [ ] Praticed Proper Risk Managment
- [ ] Set Stop Loss & Take Profit
- [ ] Trade Met Confirmations for Entry & Exit
- [ ] Followed Trading Plan

STARTING ACCOUNT BALANCE:

DATE & TIME:	PAIR:
LOT SIZE:	BUY/SELL & PIP GOAL:
STRATEGY:	WIN/LOSS:

DATE & TIME:	PAIR:
LOT SIZE:	BUY/SELL & PIP GOAL:
STRATEGY:	WIN/LOSS:

DATE & TIME:	PAIR:
LOT SIZE:	BUY/SELL & PIP GOAL:
STRATEGY:	WIN/LOSS:

DATE & TIME:	PAIR:
LOT SIZE:	BUY/SELL & PIP GOAL:
STRATEGY:	WIN/LOSS:

ENDING ACCOUNT BALANCE:

Manifest & Trade

PROOF LOG

How Do I feel?

What am I Grateful for?

What did I learn today?

What am I working towards?

What is on my wish list?

☐ Praticed Proper Risk Managment

☐ Set Stop Loss & Take Profit

☐ Trade Met Confirmations for Entry & Exit

☐ Followed Trading Plan

STARTING ACCOUNT BALANCE:

DATE & TIME:	PAIR:
LOT SIZE:	BUY/SELL & PIP GOAL:
STRATEGY:	WIN/LOSS:

DATE & TIME:	PAIR:
LOT SIZE:	BUY/SELL & PIP GOAL:
STRATEGY:	WIN/LOSS:

DATE & TIME:	PAIR:
LOT SIZE:	BUY/SELL & PIP GOAL:
STRATEGY:	WIN/LOSS:

DATE & TIME:	PAIR:
LOT SIZE:	BUY/SELL & PIP GOAL:
STRATEGY:	WIN/LOSS:

ENDING ACCOUNT BALANCE:

Manifest & Trade

PROOF LOG

How Do I feel?

What am I Grateful for?

What did I learn today?

What am I working towards?

What is on my wish list?

- [ ] Praticed Proper Risk Managment
- [ ] Set Stop Loss & Take Profit
- [ ] Trade Met Confirmations for Entry & Exit
- [ ] Followed Trading Plan

STARTING ACCOUNT BALANCE:

DATE & TIME:	PAIR:
LOT SIZE:	BUY/SELL & PIP GOAL:
STRATEGY:	WIN/LOSS:

DATE & TIME:	PAIR:
LOT SIZE:	BUY/SELL & PIP GOAL:
STRATEGY:	WIN/LOSS:

DATE & TIME:	PAIR:
LOT SIZE:	BUY/SELL & PIP GOAL:
STRATEGY:	WIN/LOSS:

DATE & TIME:	PAIR:
LOT SIZE:	BUY/SELL & PIP GOAL:
STRATEGY:	WIN/LOSS:

ENDING ACCOUNT BALANCE:

Manifest & Trade

PROOF LOG

How Do I feel?

What am I Grateful for?

What did I learn today?

What am I working towards?

What is on my wish list?

☐   Praticed Proper Risk Managment

☐   Set Stop Loss & Take Profit

☐   Trade Met Confirmations for Entry & Exit

☐   Followed Trading Plan

STARTING ACCOUNT BALANCE:

DATE & TIME:	PAIR:
LOT SIZE:	BUY/SELL & PIP GOAL:
STRATEGY:	WIN/LOSS:

DATE & TIME:	PAIR:
LOT SIZE:	BUY/SELL & PIP GOAL:
STRATEGY:	WIN/LOSS:

DATE & TIME:	PAIR:
LOT SIZE:	BUY/SELL & PIP GOAL:
STRATEGY:	WIN/LOSS:

DATE & TIME:	PAIR:
LOT SIZE:	BUY/SELL & PIP GOAL:
STRATEGY:	WIN/LOSS:

ENDING ACCOUNT BALANCE:

Manifest & Trade
PROOF LOG

How Do I feel?

What am I Grateful for?

What did I learn today?

What am I working towards?

What is on my wish list?

☐   Praticed Proper Risk Managment

☐   Set Stop Loss & Take Profit

☐   Trade Met Confirmations for Entry & Exit

☐   Followed Trading Plan

STARTING ACCOUNT BALANCE:

DATE & TIME:	PAIR:
LOT SIZE:	BUY/SELL & PIP GOAL:
STRATEGY:	WIN/LOSS:

DATE & TIME:	PAIR:
LOT SIZE:	BUY/SELL & PIP GOAL:
STRATEGY:	WIN/LOSS:

DATE & TIME:	PAIR:
LOT SIZE:	BUY/SELL & PIP GOAL:
STRATEGY:	WIN/LOSS:

DATE & TIME:	PAIR:
LOT SIZE:	BUY/SELL & PIP GOAL:
STRATEGY:	WIN/LOSS:

ENDING ACCOUNT BALANCE:

Manifest & Trade

PROOF LOG

How Do I feel?

What am I Grateful for?

What did I learn today?

What am I working towards?

What is on my wish list?

MINDSET
growth

☐ Praticed Proper Risk Managment

☐ Set Stop Loss & Take Profit

☐ Trade Met Confirmations for Entry & Exit

☐ Followed Trading Plan

DISCIPLINE
checklist

TRADING
log

STARTING ACCOUNT BALANCE:

DATE & TIME:	PAIR:
LOT SIZE:	BUY/SELL & PIP GOAL:
STRATEGY:	WIN/LOSS:

DATE & TIME:	PAIR:
LOT SIZE:	BUY/SELL & PIP GOAL:
STRATEGY:	WIN/LOSS:

DATE & TIME:	PAIR:
LOT SIZE:	BUY/SELL & PIP GOAL:
STRATEGY:	WIN/LOSS:

DATE & TIME:	PAIR:
LOT SIZE:	BUY/SELL & PIP GOAL:
STRATEGY:	WIN/LOSS:

ENDING ACCOUNT BALANCE:

Manifest & Trade

PROOF LOG

How Do I feel?

What am I Grateful for?

What did I learn today?

What am I working towards?

What is on my wish list?

- ☐ Praticed Proper Risk Managment
- ☐ Set Stop Loss & Take Profit
- ☐ Trade Met Confirmations for Entry & Exit
- ☐ Followed Trading Plan

STARTING ACCOUNT BALANCE:

DATE & TIME:	PAIR:
LOT SIZE:	BUY/SELL & PIP GOAL:
STRATEGY:	WIN/LOSS:

DATE & TIME:	PAIR:
LOT SIZE:	BUY/SELL & PIP GOAL:
STRATEGY:	WIN/LOSS:

DATE & TIME:	PAIR:
LOT SIZE:	BUY/SELL & PIP GOAL:
STRATEGY:	WIN/LOSS:

DATE & TIME:	PAIR:
LOT SIZE:	BUY/SELL & PIP GOAL:
STRATEGY:	WIN/LOSS:

ENDING ACCOUNT BALANCE:

Manifest & Trade

PROOF LOG

How Do I feel?

What am I Grateful for?

What did I learn today?

What am I working towards?

What is on my wish list?

MINDSET *growth*

☐ Praticed Proper Risk Managment

☐ Set Stop Loss & Take Profit

☐ Trade Met Confirmations for Entry & Exit

☐ Followed Trading Plan

DISCIPLINE *checklist*

TRADING *log*

STARTING ACCOUNT BALANCE:

DATE & TIME:	PAIR:
LOT SIZE:	BUY/SELL & PIP GOAL:
STRATEGY:	WIN/LOSS:

DATE & TIME:	PAIR:
LOT SIZE:	BUY/SELL & PIP GOAL:
STRATEGY:	WIN/LOSS:

DATE & TIME:	PAIR:
LOT SIZE:	BUY/SELL & PIP GOAL:
STRATEGY:	WIN/LOSS:

DATE & TIME:	PAIR:
LOT SIZE:	BUY/SELL & PIP GOAL:
STRATEGY:	WIN/LOSS:

ENDING ACCOUNT BALANCE:

Manifest & Trade

PROOF LOG

How Do I feel?

What am I Grateful for?

What did I learn today?

What am I working towards?

What is on my wish list?

- ☐ Praticed Proper Risk Managment
- ☐ Set Stop Loss & Take Profit
- ☐ Trade Met Confirmations for Entry & Exit
- ☐ Followed Trading Plan

STARTING ACCOUNT BALANCE:

DATE & TIME:	PAIR:
LOT SIZE:	BUY/SELL & PIP GOAL:
STRATEGY:	WIN/LOSS:

DATE & TIME:	PAIR:
LOT SIZE:	BUY/SELL & PIP GOAL:
STRATEGY:	WIN/LOSS:

DATE & TIME:	PAIR:
LOT SIZE:	BUY/SELL & PIP GOAL:
STRATEGY:	WIN/LOSS:

DATE & TIME:	PAIR:
LOT SIZE:	BUY/SELL & PIP GOAL:
STRATEGY:	WIN/LOSS:

ENDING ACCOUNT BALANCE:

Manifest & Trade

PROOF LOG

How Do I feel?

What am I Grateful for?

What did I learn today?

What am I working towards?

What is on my wish list?

MINDSET
growth

- [ ] Praticed Proper Risk Managment
- [ ] Set Stop Loss & Take Profit
- [ ] Trade Met Confirmations for Entry & Exit
- [ ] Followed Trading Plan

DISCIPLINE
checklist

TRADING
log

STARTING ACCOUNT BALANCE:

DATE & TIME:	PAIR:
LOT SIZE:	BUY/SELL & PIP GOAL:
STRATEGY:	WIN/LOSS:

DATE & TIME:	PAIR:
LOT SIZE:	BUY/SELL & PIP GOAL:
STRATEGY:	WIN/LOSS:

DATE & TIME:	PAIR:
LOT SIZE:	BUY/SELL & PIP GOAL:
STRATEGY:	WIN/LOSS:

DATE & TIME:	PAIR:
LOT SIZE:	BUY/SELL & PIP GOAL:
STRATEGY:	WIN/LOSS:

ENDING ACCOUNT BALANCE:

Manifest & Trade

PROOF LOG

How Do I feel?

What am I Grateful for?

What did I learn today?

What am I working towards?

What is on my wish list?

MINDSET
growth

- [ ] Praticed Proper Risk Managment
- [ ] Set Stop Loss & Take Profit
- [ ] Trade Met Confirmations for Entry & Exit
- [ ] Followed Trading Plan

DISCIPLINE
checklist

TRADING
log

STARTING ACCOUNT BALANCE:

DATE & TIME:	PAIR:
LOT SIZE:	BUY/SELL & PIP GOAL:
STRATEGY:	WIN/LOSS:

DATE & TIME:	PAIR:
LOT SIZE:	BUY/SELL & PIP GOAL:
STRATEGY:	WIN/LOSS:

DATE & TIME:	PAIR:
LOT SIZE:	BUY/SELL & PIP GOAL:
STRATEGY:	WIN/LOSS:

DATE & TIME:	PAIR:
LOT SIZE:	BUY/SELL & PIP GOAL:
STRATEGY:	WIN/LOSS:

ENDING ACCOUNT BALANCE:

Manifest & Trade

PROOF LOG

How Do I feel?

What am I Grateful for?

What did I learn today?

What am I working towards?

What is on my wish list?

- [ ] Praticed Proper Risk Managment
- [ ] Set Stop Loss & Take Profit
- [ ] Trade Met Confirmations for Entry & Exit
- [ ] Followed Trading Plan

STARTING ACCOUNT BALANCE:

DATE & TIME:	PAIR:
LOT SIZE:	BUY/SELL & PIP GOAL:
STRATEGY:	WIN/LOSS:

DATE & TIME:	PAIR:
LOT SIZE:	BUY/SELL & PIP GOAL:
STRATEGY:	WIN/LOSS:

DATE & TIME:	PAIR:
LOT SIZE:	BUY/SELL & PIP GOAL:
STRATEGY:	WIN/LOSS:

DATE & TIME:	PAIR:
LOT SIZE:	BUY/SELL & PIP GOAL:
STRATEGY:	WIN/LOSS:

ENDING ACCOUNT BALANCE:

Manifest & Trade

PROOF LOG

How Do I feel?

What am I Grateful for?

What did I learn today?

What am I working towards?

What is on my wish list?

- [ ] Praticed Proper Risk Managment
- [ ] Set Stop Loss & Take Profit
- [ ] Trade Met Confirmations for Entry & Exit
- [ ] Followed Trading Plan

STARTING ACCOUNT BALANCE:

DATE & TIME:	PAIR:
LOT SIZE:	BUY/SELL & PIP GOAL:
STRATEGY:	WIN/LOSS:

DATE & TIME:	PAIR:
LOT SIZE:	BUY/SELL & PIP GOAL:
STRATEGY:	WIN/LOSS:

DATE & TIME:	PAIR:
LOT SIZE:	BUY/SELL & PIP GOAL:
STRATEGY:	WIN/LOSS:

DATE & TIME:	PAIR:
LOT SIZE:	BUY/SELL & PIP GOAL:
STRATEGY:	WIN/LOSS:

ENDING ACCOUNT BALANCE:

Manifest & Trade

PROOF LOG

How Do I feel?

What am I Grateful for?

What did I learn today?

What am I working towards?

What is on my wish list?

☐ Praticed Proper Risk Managment

☐ Set Stop Loss & Take Profit

☐ Trade Met Confirmations for Entry & Exit

☐ Followed Trading Plan

STARTING ACCOUNT BALANCE:

DATE & TIME: _____ PAIR: _____

LOT SIZE: _____ BUY/SELL & PIP GOAL: _____

STRATEGY: _____ WIN/LOSS: _____

DATE & TIME: _____ PAIR: _____

LOT SIZE: _____ BUY/SELL & PIP GOAL: _____

STRATEGY: _____ WIN/LOSS: _____

DATE & TIME: _____ PAIR: _____

LOT SIZE: _____ BUY/SELL & PIP GOAL: _____

STRATEGY: _____ WIN/LOSS: _____

DATE & TIME: _____ PAIR: _____

LOT SIZE: _____ BUY/SELL & PIP GOAL: _____

STRATEGY: _____ WIN/LOSS: _____

ENDING ACCOUNT BALANCE:

Manifest & Trade

PROOF LOG

How Do I feel?

What am I Grateful for?

What did I learn today?

What am I working towards?

What is on my wish list?

☐ Praticed Proper Risk Managment

☐ Set Stop Loss & Take Profit

☐ Trade Met Confirmations for Entry & Exit

☐ Followed Trading Plan

STARTING ACCOUNT BALANCE:

DATE & TIME:	PAIR:
LOT SIZE:	BUY/SELL & PIP GOAL:
STRATEGY:	WIN/LOSS:

DATE & TIME:	PAIR:
LOT SIZE:	BUY/SELL & PIP GOAL:
STRATEGY:	WIN/LOSS:

DATE & TIME:	PAIR:
LOT SIZE:	BUY/SELL & PIP GOAL:
STRATEGY:	WIN/LOSS:

DATE & TIME:	PAIR:
LOT SIZE:	BUY/SELL & PIP GOAL:
STRATEGY:	WIN/LOSS:

ENDING ACCOUNT BALANCE:

Manifest & Trade

PROOF LOG

How Do I feel?

What am I Grateful for?

What did I learn today?

What am I working towards?

What is on my wish list?

- [ ] Praticed Proper Risk Managment
- [ ] Set Stop Loss & Take Profit
- [ ] Trade Met Confirmations for Entry & Exit
- [ ] Followed Trading Plan

STARTING ACCOUNT BALANCE:

DATE & TIME:	PAIR:
LOT SIZE:	BUY/SELL & PIP GOAL:
STRATEGY:	WIN/LOSS:

DATE & TIME:	PAIR:
LOT SIZE:	BUY/SELL & PIP GOAL:
STRATEGY:	WIN/LOSS:

DATE & TIME:	PAIR:
LOT SIZE:	BUY/SELL & PIP GOAL:
STRATEGY:	WIN/LOSS:

DATE & TIME:	PAIR:
LOT SIZE:	BUY/SELL & PIP GOAL:
STRATEGY:	WIN/LOSS:

ENDING ACCOUNT BALANCE:

Manifest & Trade

PROOF LOG

How Do I feel?

What am I Grateful for?

What did I learn today?

What am I working towards?

What is on my wish list?

- [ ] Praticed Proper Risk Managment
- [ ] Set Stop Loss & Take Profit
- [ ] Trade Met Confirmations for Entry & Exit
- [ ] Followed Trading Plan

STARTING ACCOUNT BALANCE:

DATE & TIME:	PAIR:
LOT SIZE:	BUY/SELL & PIP GOAL:
STRATEGY:	WIN/LOSS:

DATE & TIME:	PAIR:
LOT SIZE:	BUY/SELL & PIP GOAL:
STRATEGY:	WIN/LOSS:

DATE & TIME:	PAIR:
LOT SIZE:	BUY/SELL & PIP GOAL:
STRATEGY:	WIN/LOSS:

DATE & TIME:	PAIR:
LOT SIZE:	BUY/SELL & PIP GOAL:
STRATEGY:	WIN/LOSS:

ENDING ACCOUNT BALANCE:

Manifest & Trade

PROOF LOG

How Do I feel?

What am I Grateful for?

What did I learn today?

What am I working towards?

What is on my wish list?

☐ Praticed Proper Risk Managment

☐ Set Stop Loss & Take Profit

☐ Trade Met Confirmations for Entry & Exit

☐ Followed Trading Plan

STARTING ACCOUNT BALANCE:

DATE & TIME:	PAIR:
LOT SIZE:	BUY/SELL & PIP GOAL:
STRATEGY:	WIN/LOSS:

DATE & TIME:	PAIR:
LOT SIZE:	BUY/SELL & PIP GOAL:
STRATEGY:	WIN/LOSS:

DATE & TIME:	PAIR:
LOT SIZE:	BUY/SELL & PIP GOAL:
STRATEGY:	WIN/LOSS:

DATE & TIME:	PAIR:
LOT SIZE:	BUY/SELL & PIP GOAL:
STRATEGY:	WIN/LOSS:

ENDING ACCOUNT BALANCE:

Manifest & Trade

PROOF LOG

How Do I feel?

What am I Grateful for?

What did I learn today?

What am I working towards?

What is on my wish list?

- [ ] Praticed Proper Risk Managment
- [ ] Set Stop Loss & Take Profit
- [ ] Trade Met Confirmations for Entry & Exit
- [ ] Followed Trading Plan

STARTING ACCOUNT BALANCE:

DATE & TIME:	PAIR:
LOT SIZE:	BUY/SELL & PIP GOAL:
STRATEGY:	WIN/LOSS:

DATE & TIME:	PAIR:
LOT SIZE:	BUY/SELL & PIP GOAL:
STRATEGY:	WIN/LOSS:

DATE & TIME:	PAIR:
LOT SIZE:	BUY/SELL & PIP GOAL:
STRATEGY:	WIN/LOSS:

DATE & TIME:	PAIR:
LOT SIZE:	BUY/SELL & PIP GOAL:
STRATEGY:	WIN/LOSS:

ENDING ACCOUNT BALANCE:

Manifest & Trade

PROOF LOG

How Do I feel?

What am I Grateful for?

What did I learn today?

What am I working towards?

What is on my wish list?

☐ Praticed Proper Risk Managment

☐ Set Stop Loss & Take Profit

☐ Trade Met Confirmations for Entry & Exit

☐ Followed Trading Plan

MINDSET
growth

DISCIPLINE
checklist

TRADING
log

STARTING ACCOUNT BALANCE:

DATE & TIME:	PAIR:
LOT SIZE:	BUY/SELL & PIP GOAL:
STRATEGY:	WIN/LOSS:

DATE & TIME:	PAIR:
LOT SIZE:	BUY/SELL & PIP GOAL:
STRATEGY:	WIN/LOSS:

DATE & TIME:	PAIR:
LOT SIZE:	BUY/SELL & PIP GOAL:
STRATEGY:	WIN/LOSS:

DATE & TIME:	PAIR:
LOT SIZE:	BUY/SELL & PIP GOAL:
STRATEGY:	WIN/LOSS:

ENDING ACCOUNT BALANCE:

Manifest & Trade

PROOF LOG

How Do I feel?

What am I Grateful for?

What did I learn today?

What am I working towards?

What is on my wish list?

- [ ] Praticed Proper Risk Managment
- [ ] Set Stop Loss & Take Profit
- [ ] Trade Met Confirmations for Entry & Exit
- [ ] Followed Trading Plan

STARTING ACCOUNT BALANCE:

DATE & TIME:	PAIR:
LOT SIZE:	BUY/SELL & PIP GOAL:
STRATEGY:	WIN/LOSS:

DATE & TIME:	PAIR:
LOT SIZE:	BUY/SELL & PIP GOAL:
STRATEGY:	WIN/LOSS:

DATE & TIME:	PAIR:
LOT SIZE:	BUY/SELL & PIP GOAL:
STRATEGY:	WIN/LOSS:

DATE & TIME:	PAIR:
LOT SIZE:	BUY/SELL & PIP GOAL:
STRATEGY:	WIN/LOSS:

ENDING ACCOUNT BALANCE:

Manifest & Trade

PROOF LOG

How Do I feel?

What am I Grateful for?

What did I learn today?

What am I working towards?

What is on my wish list?

MINDSET
growth

- [ ] Praticed Proper Risk Managment
- [ ] Set Stop Loss & Take Profit
- [ ] Trade Met Confirmations for Entry & Exit
- [ ] Followed Trading Plan

DISCIPLINE
checklist

TRADING
log

STARTING ACCOUNT BALANCE:

DATE & TIME:	PAIR:
LOT SIZE:	BUY/SELL & PIP GOAL:
STRATEGY:	WIN/LOSS:

DATE & TIME:	PAIR:
LOT SIZE:	BUY/SELL & PIP GOAL:
STRATEGY:	WIN/LOSS:

DATE & TIME:	PAIR:
LOT SIZE:	BUY/SELL & PIP GOAL:
STRATEGY:	WIN/LOSS:

DATE & TIME:	PAIR:
LOT SIZE:	BUY/SELL & PIP GOAL:
STRATEGY:	WIN/LOSS:

ENDING ACCOUNT BALANCE:

Manifest & Trade

How Do I feel?

What am I Grateful for?

What did I learn today?

What am I working towards?

What is on my wish list?

growth

☐   Praticed Proper Risk Managment

☐   Set Stop Loss & Take Profit

☐   Trade Met Confirmations for Entry & Exit

☐   Followed Trading Plan

checklist

STARTING ACCOUNT BALANCE:

TRADING
log

DATE & TIME:	PAIR:
LOT SIZE:	BUY/SELL & PIP GOAL:
STRATEGY:	WIN/LOSS:

DATE & TIME:	PAIR:
LOT SIZE:	BUY/SELL & PIP GOAL:
STRATEGY:	WIN/LOSS:

DATE & TIME:	PAIR:
LOT SIZE:	BUY/SELL & PIP GOAL:
STRATEGY:	WIN/LOSS:

DATE & TIME:	PAIR:
LOT SIZE:	BUY/SELL & PIP GOAL:
STRATEGY:	WIN/LOSS:

ENDING ACCOUNT BALANCE:

Manifest & Trade

PROOF LOG

How Do I feel?

What am I Grateful for?

What did I learn today?

What am I working towards?

What is on my wish list?

- [ ] Praticed Proper Risk Managment
- [ ] Set Stop Loss & Take Profit
- [ ] Trade Met Confirmations for Entry & Exit
- [ ] Followed Trading Plan

STARTING ACCOUNT BALANCE:

DATE & TIME:	PAIR:
LOT SIZE:	BUY/SELL & PIP GOAL:
STRATEGY:	WIN/LOSS:

DATE & TIME:	PAIR:
LOT SIZE:	BUY/SELL & PIP GOAL:
STRATEGY:	WIN/LOSS:

DATE & TIME:	PAIR:
LOT SIZE:	BUY/SELL & PIP GOAL:
STRATEGY:	WIN/LOSS:

DATE & TIME:	PAIR:
LOT SIZE:	BUY/SELL & PIP GOAL:
STRATEGY:	WIN/LOSS:

ENDING ACCOUNT BALANCE:

Manifest & Trade

PROOF LOG

How Do I feel?

What am I Grateful for?

What did I learn today?

What am I working towards?

What is on my wish list?

MINDSET
growth

- ☐ Praticed Proper Risk Managment
- ☐ Set Stop Loss & Take Profit
- ☐ Trade Met Confirmations for Entry & Exit
- ☐ Followed Trading Plan

DISCIPLINE
checklist

TRADING
log

STARTING ACCOUNT BALANCE:

DATE & TIME:	PAIR:
LOT SIZE:	BUY/SELL & PIP GOAL:
STRATEGY:	WIN/LOSS:

DATE & TIME:	PAIR:
LOT SIZE:	BUY/SELL & PIP GOAL:
STRATEGY:	WIN/LOSS:

DATE & TIME:	PAIR:
LOT SIZE:	BUY/SELL & PIP GOAL:
STRATEGY:	WIN/LOSS:

DATE & TIME:	PAIR:
LOT SIZE:	BUY/SELL & PIP GOAL:
STRATEGY:	WIN/LOSS:

ENDING ACCOUNT BALANCE:

Manifest & Trade
PROOF LOG

How Do I feel?

What am I Grateful for?

What did I learn today?

What am I working towards?

What is on my wish list?

☐	Praticed Proper Risk Managment
☐	Set Stop Loss & Take Profit
☐	Trade Met Confirmations for Entry & Exit
☐	Followed Trading Plan

MINDSET
growth

DISCIPLINE
checklist

TRADING
log

STARTING ACCOUNT BALANCE:

DATE & TIME:

PAIR:

LOT SIZE:

BUY/SELL & PIP GOAL:

STRATEGY:

WIN/LOSS:

DATE & TIME:

PAIR:

LOT SIZE:

BUY/SELL & PIP GOAL:

STRATEGY:

WIN/LOSS:

DATE & TIME:

PAIR:

LOT SIZE:

BUY/SELL & PIP GOAL:

STRATEGY:

WIN/LOSS:

DATE & TIME:

PAIR:

LOT SIZE:

BUY/SELL & PIP GOAL:

STRATEGY:

WIN/LOSS:

ENDING ACCOUNT BALANCE:

Manifest & Trade

How Do I feel?

What am I Grateful for?

What did I learn today?

What am I working towards?

What is on my wish list?

MINDSET
growth

☐ Praticed Proper Risk Managment

☐ Set Stop Loss & Take Profit

☐ Trade Met Confirmations for Entry & Exit

☐ Followed Trading Plan

DISCIPLINE
checklist

TRADING
log

STARTING ACCOUNT BALANCE:

DATE & TIME:	PAIR:
LOT SIZE:	BUY/SELL & PIP GOAL:
STRATEGY:	WIN/LOSS:

DATE & TIME:	PAIR:
LOT SIZE:	BUY/SELL & PIP GOAL:
STRATEGY:	WIN/LOSS:

DATE & TIME:	PAIR:
LOT SIZE:	BUY/SELL & PIP GOAL:
STRATEGY:	WIN/LOSS:

DATE & TIME:	PAIR:
LOT SIZE:	BUY/SELL & PIP GOAL:
STRATEGY:	WIN/LOSS:

ENDING ACCOUNT BALANCE:

Manifest & Trade

PROOF LOG

How Do I feel?

What am I Grateful for?

What did I learn today?

What am I working towards?

What is on my wish list?

☐ Praticed Proper Risk Managment

☐ Set Stop Loss & Take Profit

☐ Trade Met Confirmations for Entry & Exit

☐ Followed Trading Plan

STARTING ACCOUNT BALANCE:

DATE & TIME:	PAIR:
LOT SIZE:	BUY/SELL & PIP GOAL:
STRATEGY:	WIN/LOSS:

DATE & TIME:	PAIR:
LOT SIZE:	BUY/SELL & PIP GOAL:
STRATEGY:	WIN/LOSS:

DATE & TIME:	PAIR:
LOT SIZE:	BUY/SELL & PIP GOAL:
STRATEGY:	WIN/LOSS:

DATE & TIME:	PAIR:
LOT SIZE:	BUY/SELL & PIP GOAL:
STRATEGY:	WIN/LOSS:

ENDING ACCOUNT BALANCE:

Manifest & Trade

PROOF LOG

How Do I feel?

What am I Grateful for?

What did I learn today?

What am I working towards?

What is on my wish list?

- ☐ Praticed Proper Risk Managment
- ☐ Set Stop Loss & Take Profit
- ☐ Trade Met Confirmations for Entry & Exit
- ☐ Followed Trading Plan

STARTING ACCOUNT BALANCE:

DATE & TIME:	PAIR:
LOT SIZE:	BUY/SELL & PIP GOAL:
STRATEGY:	WIN/LOSS:

DATE & TIME:	PAIR:
LOT SIZE:	BUY/SELL & PIP GOAL:
STRATEGY:	WIN/LOSS:

DATE & TIME:	PAIR:
LOT SIZE:	BUY/SELL & PIP GOAL:
STRATEGY:	WIN/LOSS:

DATE & TIME:	PAIR:
LOT SIZE:	BUY/SELL & PIP GOAL:
STRATEGY:	WIN/LOSS:

ENDING ACCOUNT BALANCE:

Manifest & Trade

PROOF LOG

How Do I feel?

What am I Grateful for?

What did I learn today?

What am I working towards?

What is on my wish list?

- ☐ Praticed Proper Risk Managment
- ☐ Set Stop Loss & Take Profit
- ☐ Trade Met Confirmations for Entry & Exit
- ☐ Followed Trading Plan

STARTING ACCOUNT BALANCE:

DATE & TIME:	PAIR:
LOT SIZE:	BUY/SELL & PIP GOAL:
STRATEGY:	WIN/LOSS:

DATE & TIME:	PAIR:
LOT SIZE:	BUY/SELL & PIP GOAL:
STRATEGY:	WIN/LOSS:

DATE & TIME:	PAIR:
LOT SIZE:	BUY/SELL & PIP GOAL:
STRATEGY:	WIN/LOSS:

DATE & TIME:	PAIR:
LOT SIZE:	BUY/SELL & PIP GOAL:
STRATEGY:	WIN/LOSS:

ENDING ACCOUNT BALANCE:

Manifest & Trade

PROOF LOG

How Do I feel?

What am I Grateful for?

What did I learn today?

What am I working towards?

What is on my wish list?

☐ Praticed Proper Risk Managment

☐ Set Stop Loss & Take Profit

☐ Trade Met Confirmations for Entry & Exit

☐ Followed Trading Plan

STARTING ACCOUNT BALANCE:

DATE & TIME:	PAIR:
LOT SIZE:	BUY/SELL & PIP GOAL:
STRATEGY:	WIN/LOSS:

DATE & TIME:	PAIR:
LOT SIZE:	BUY/SELL & PIP GOAL:
STRATEGY:	WIN/LOSS:

DATE & TIME:	PAIR:
LOT SIZE:	BUY/SELL & PIP GOAL:
STRATEGY:	WIN/LOSS:

DATE & TIME:	PAIR:
LOT SIZE:	BUY/SELL & PIP GOAL:
STRATEGY:	WIN/LOSS:

ENDING ACCOUNT BALANCE:

Manifest & Trade

PROOF LOG

How Do I feel?

What am I Grateful for?

What did I learn today?

What am I working towards?

What is on my wish list?

☐ Praticed Proper Risk Managment

☐ Set Stop Loss & Take Profit

☐ Trade Met Confirmations for Entry & Exit

☐ Followed Trading Plan

STARTING ACCOUNT BALANCE:

DATE & TIME:	PAIR:
LOT SIZE:	BUY/SELL & PIP GOAL:
STRATEGY:	WIN/LOSS:

DATE & TIME:	PAIR:
LOT SIZE:	BUY/SELL & PIP GOAL:
STRATEGY:	WIN/LOSS:

DATE & TIME:	PAIR:
LOT SIZE:	BUY/SELL & PIP GOAL:
STRATEGY:	WIN/LOSS:

DATE & TIME:	PAIR:
LOT SIZE:	BUY/SELL & PIP GOAL:
STRATEGY:	WIN/LOSS:

ENDING ACCOUNT BALANCE:

Manifest & Trade

PROOF LOG

How Do I feel?

What am I Grateful for?

What did I learn today?

What am I working towards?

What is on my wish list?

☐ Praticed Proper Risk Managment

☐ Set Stop Loss & Take Profit

☐ Trade Met Confirmations for Entry & Exit

☐ Followed Trading Plan

STARTING ACCOUNT BALANCE:

DATE & TIME:	PAIR:
LOT SIZE:	BUY/SELL & PIP GOAL:
STRATEGY:	WIN/LOSS:

DATE & TIME:	PAIR:
LOT SIZE:	BUY/SELL & PIP GOAL:
STRATEGY:	WIN/LOSS:

DATE & TIME:	PAIR:
LOT SIZE:	BUY/SELL & PIP GOAL:
STRATEGY:	WIN/LOSS:

DATE & TIME:	PAIR:
LOT SIZE:	BUY/SELL & PIP GOAL:
STRATEGY:	WIN/LOSS:

ENDING ACCOUNT BALANCE:

Manifest & Trade

PROOF LOG

How Do I feel?

What am I Grateful for?

What did I learn today?

What am I working towards?

What is on my wish list?

MINDSET
growth

- ☐ Praticed Proper Risk Managment
- ☐ Set Stop Loss & Take Profit
- ☐ Trade Met Confirmations for Entry & Exit
- ☐ Followed Trading Plan

DISCIPLINE
checklist

TRADING
log

STARTING ACCOUNT BALANCE:

DATE & TIME:	PAIR:
LOT SIZE:	BUY/SELL & PIP GOAL:
STRATEGY:	WIN/LOSS:

DATE & TIME:	PAIR:
LOT SIZE:	BUY/SELL & PIP GOAL:
STRATEGY:	WIN/LOSS:

DATE & TIME:	PAIR:
LOT SIZE:	BUY/SELL & PIP GOAL:
STRATEGY:	WIN/LOSS:

DATE & TIME:	PAIR:
LOT SIZE:	BUY/SELL & PIP GOAL:
STRATEGY:	WIN/LOSS:

ENDING ACCOUNT BALANCE:

Manifest & Trade

PROOF LOG

How Do I feel?

What am I Grateful for?

What did I learn today?

What am I working towards?

What is on my wish list?

MINDSET
growth

- [ ] Praticed Proper Risk Managment
- [ ] Set Stop Loss & Take Profit
- [ ] Trade Met Confirmations for Entry & Exit
- [ ] Followed Trading Plan

DISCIPLINE
checklist

STARTING ACCOUNT BALANCE:

TRADING
log

DATE & TIME:	PAIR:
LOT SIZE:	BUY/SELL & PIP GOAL:
STRATEGY:	WIN/LOSS:

DATE & TIME:	PAIR:
LOT SIZE:	BUY/SELL & PIP GOAL:
STRATEGY:	WIN/LOSS:

DATE & TIME:	PAIR:
LOT SIZE:	BUY/SELL & PIP GOAL:
STRATEGY:	WIN/LOSS:

DATE & TIME:	PAIR:
LOT SIZE:	BUY/SELL & PIP GOAL:
STRATEGY:	WIN/LOSS:

ENDING ACCOUNT BALANCE:

Manifest & Trade

PROOF LOG

How Do I feel?

What am I Grateful for?

What did I learn today?

What am I working towards?

What is on my wish list?

☐   Praticed Proper Risk Managment

☐   Set Stop Loss & Take Profit

☐   Trade Met Confirmations for Entry & Exit

☐   Followed Trading Plan

STARTING ACCOUNT BALANCE: _____

DATE & TIME:	PAIR:
LOT SIZE:	BUY/SELL & PIP GOAL:
STRATEGY:	WIN/LOSS:

DATE & TIME:	PAIR:
LOT SIZE:	BUY/SELL & PIP GOAL:
STRATEGY:	WIN/LOSS:

DATE & TIME:	PAIR:
LOT SIZE:	BUY/SELL & PIP GOAL:
STRATEGY:	WIN/LOSS:

DATE & TIME:	PAIR:
LOT SIZE:	BUY/SELL & PIP GOAL:
STRATEGY:	WIN/LOSS:

ENDING ACCOUNT BALANCE:

Manifest & Trade

How Do I feel?

What am I Grateful for?

What did I learn today?

What am I working towards?

What is on my wish list?

MINDSET
growth

- ☐ Praticed Proper Risk Managment
- ☐ Set Stop Loss & Take Profit
- ☐ Trade Met Confirmations for Entry & Exit
- ☐ Followed Trading Plan

DISCIPLINE
checklist

STARTING ACCOUNT BALANCE:

TRADING
log

DATE & TIME:	PAIR:
LOT SIZE:	BUY/SELL & PIP GOAL:
STRATEGY:	WIN/LOSS:

DATE & TIME:	PAIR:
LOT SIZE:	BUY/SELL & PIP GOAL:
STRATEGY:	WIN/LOSS:

DATE & TIME:	PAIR:
LOT SIZE:	BUY/SELL & PIP GOAL:
STRATEGY:	WIN/LOSS:

DATE & TIME:	PAIR:
LOT SIZE:	BUY/SELL & PIP GOAL:
STRATEGY:	WIN/LOSS:

ENDING ACCOUNT BALANCE:

Manifest & Trade

PROOF LOG

How Do I feel?

What am I Grateful for?

What did I learn today?

What am I working towards?

What is on my wish list?

- ☐ Praticed Proper Risk Managment
- ☐ Set Stop Loss & Take Profit
- ☐ Trade Met Confirmations for Entry & Exit
- ☐ Followed Trading Plan

STARTING ACCOUNT BALANCE:

DATE & TIME:	PAIR:
LOT SIZE:	BUY/SELL & PIP GOAL:
STRATEGY:	WIN/LOSS:

DATE & TIME:	PAIR:
LOT SIZE:	BUY/SELL & PIP GOAL:
STRATEGY:	WIN/LOSS:

DATE & TIME:	PAIR:
LOT SIZE:	BUY/SELL & PIP GOAL:
STRATEGY:	WIN/LOSS:

DATE & TIME:	PAIR:
LOT SIZE:	BUY/SELL & PIP GOAL:
STRATEGY:	WIN/LOSS:

ENDING ACCOUNT BALANCE:

Manifest & Trade

PROOF LOG

How Do I feel?

What am I Grateful for?

What did I learn today?

What am I working towards?

What is on my wish list?

MINDSET
growth

☐ Praticed Proper Risk Managment

☐ Set Stop Loss & Take Profit

☐ Trade Met Confirmations for Entry & Exit

☐ Followed Trading Plan

DISCIPLINE
checklist

TRADING
log

STARTING ACCOUNT BALANCE:

DATE & TIME:	PAIR:
LOT SIZE:	BUY/SELL & PIP GOAL:
STRATEGY:	WIN/LOSS:

DATE & TIME:	PAIR:
LOT SIZE:	BUY/SELL & PIP GOAL:
STRATEGY:	WIN/LOSS:

DATE & TIME:	PAIR:
LOT SIZE:	BUY/SELL & PIP GOAL:
STRATEGY:	WIN/LOSS:

DATE & TIME:	PAIR:
LOT SIZE:	BUY/SELL & PIP GOAL:
STRATEGY:	WIN/LOSS:

ENDING ACCOUNT BALANCE:

Manifest & Trade

PROOF LOG

How Do I feel?

What am I Grateful for?

What did I learn today?

What am I working towards?

What is on my wish list?

MINDSET
growth

- [ ] Praticed Proper Risk Managment
- [ ] Set Stop Loss & Take Profit
- [ ] Trade Met Confirmations for Entry & Exit
- [ ] Followed Trading Plan

DISCIPLINE
checklist

TRADING
log

STARTING ACCOUNT BALANCE:

DATE & TIME:	PAIR:
LOT SIZE:	BUY/SELL & PIP GOAL:
STRATEGY:	WIN/LOSS:

DATE & TIME:	PAIR:
LOT SIZE:	BUY/SELL & PIP GOAL:
STRATEGY:	WIN/LOSS:

DATE & TIME:	PAIR:
LOT SIZE:	BUY/SELL & PIP GOAL:
STRATEGY:	WIN/LOSS:

DATE & TIME:	PAIR:
LOT SIZE:	BUY/SELL & PIP GOAL:
STRATEGY:	WIN/LOSS:

ENDING ACCOUNT BALANCE:

Manifest & Trade

PROOF LOG

How Do I feel?

What am I Grateful for?

What did I learn today?

What am I working towards?

What is on my wish list?

MINDSET
growth

- [ ] Praticed Proper Risk Managment
- [ ] Set Stop Loss & Take Profit
- [ ] Trade Met Confirmations for Entry & Exit
- [ ] Followed Trading Plan

DISCIPLINE
checklist

TRADING
log

STARTING ACCOUNT BALANCE:

DATE & TIME:	PAIR:
LOT SIZE:	BUY/SELL & PIP GOAL:
STRATEGY:	WIN/LOSS:

DATE & TIME:	PAIR:
LOT SIZE:	BUY/SELL & PIP GOAL:
STRATEGY:	WIN/LOSS:

DATE & TIME:	PAIR:
LOT SIZE:	BUY/SELL & PIP GOAL:
STRATEGY:	WIN/LOSS:

DATE & TIME:	PAIR:
LOT SIZE:	BUY/SELL & PIP GOAL:
STRATEGY:	WIN/LOSS:

ENDING ACCOUNT BALANCE:

www.ingramcontent.com/pod-product-compliance
Lightning Source LLC
Chambersburg PA
CBHW070406220526
45467CB00001B/489